Not So Bright Side

Madilyn Gonzalez

BookLeaf
Publishing

India | USA | UK

Presentation by *BookLeaf Publishing*

Web: www.bookleafpub.com

E-mail: info@bookleafpub.com

ISBN: 9789363319967

First edition 2024

Papa, one thing and one thing only, banana tank top.

Mama, look a buffalo!

ACKNOWLEDGEMENT

Along the way, there have been some standout teachers that have influenced me and inspired me to write.

Ms. Saunders, my elementary school English teacher, helped me enrich my reading skills and instilled a love for reading.

Ms. Lara, my middle school English teacher, showed unwavering belief in me, and kept my interests alive.

And lastly, Brazilian JiuJitsu Professor Marcelo Herz, that taught me to never give up, when under pressure.

PREFACE

I really don't know what to write here,
but I do hope that you enjoy these words I have
crafted for you.

I Can't Sleep

Thoughts running through my head,
Staring at the celling in my bed;
Seconds, minutes, and hours pass by,
I try, try, and try.

Go to sleep,
I tried the usual counting sheep;
Get some rest,
If you don't, you'll be a mess.

Turned to one side of the bed,
Thoughts still running through my head;
Turned to the other,
Sleep, Sleep, Sleep, I muttered.

I Thought About You

Every time I think about you, I cry,
Bringing myself to say the final goodbye;
My heart hurts,
Thoughts about you still lurk.

I lost my spark,
You were light and now it's dark;
I loved you,
Did you love me too?

You said you did,
But at the end of the day, we were just kids;
First loves do stink,
It stains you like ink.

The laughter and smiles we shared,
I knew you cared;
I miss you,
I know you do too.

The Bright Side of Being Alone

In a world that craves constant connection,
The silence can feel like a heavy affliction.
Within the stillness, a treasure lies,
A chance to reconnect, to our own surprise.

For when we are alone, the noise fades away,
and we're left with ourselves, to find our way.
No distractions to cloud, no voices to sway,
Just pure essence of our own inner play.

In this solitary space, we can truly hear,
The whispers of our heart, the thoughts that are
dear.
We can delve into our dreams, our passions, our
fears,
And find the strength to face them, without any
tears.

The gift of solitude is not one to be feared,
but a chance to grow, to become more revered.
For in the quiet moments, we find our true self,
Unencumbered by others, just our own mental
wealth.

The embrace, the beauty of being alone,
The chance to reflect, to make our own thoughts
our own.
For in this sacred space, we'll find the clarity we
seek,
And emerge stronger, wiser, our spirits more
unique.

Maybe in Another Life

In the quiet moments, when the world fades
away,
I find myself wondering, what if it were a
different day?
What if the path I chose had taken a different
turn?
Would the lessons I've learned still have the
same concern?

Maybe in another life, I'd be someone else
entirely,
living a different story, one that's not so familiar
to me.
Perhaps I'd be a dreamer, chasing the stars
above,
Or a wanderer, seeking adventure, with an open
heart to love.

In this existence, would I still feel the same?
The joys and the sorrows, the triumphs and the
pain?
Or would my perspective be entirely new and
true?
Seeing the world through a lens that's not quite
like the one I knew?

The what-ifs and the maybes, they dance in my mind,
Reminding me that life is not set in stone, but intertwined.
That in every moment, there's a path to be made,
A path to be forged, a legacy to be laid.

So, I ponder this notion, of another life, another me,
Wondering if the grass is truly greener, or if it's just fantasy.
But in the end, I know that this life is the one I've been given,
And I'll make the most of it, with a heart that's truly driven.

For in this existence with all its twists and turns,
I've learned lessons that no other life could ever learn.
And though the "what-ifs" may linger, like a gentle breeze,
I'll embrace the present, and all the joy it brings to me.

Do All Good Things Come to an End?

The sun sets, the day fades away.
All that is bright cannot forever stay.
The blooming flower wilts and dies,
It's beauty a mere fleeting prize.

Laughter echoes, then falls silent,
Joyous moments cannot be permanent.
Friendship forged, bonds that once were strong,
Slowly unravel, their time short.

Success achieved, accolades earned,
Laurels worn, then swiftly overturned.
Wealth amassed, power held in hand,
Slips away, like grains of sand.

For all that is good, all that is fair,
Faces the cruel truth, the end is there.
Nothing lasts forever 'neath the sky,
All good things, in time, must die.

Yet in this truth, a lesson lies-
Cherish each moment before it flies.
For though good may fade away,
Its memory can light another day.

Thinking Too Much

The mind, a restless, whirring machine,
Churning thoughts, an endless stream.
Pondering, analyzing, dissecting each part,
Seeking answers that tear at the heart.

What if this happens? What if that's true?
Endless scenarios, the mind runs askew.
Trapped in a labyrinth of "what-ifs" and
"maybes",
Drowning in a sea of anxious maybes.

The simplest tasks become complex and fraught,
Decisions delayed, by overthinking caught.
Paralyzed by the weight of too many thoughts,
Unable to act, the mind's progress halts.

A cacophony of voices, each vying for sway,
Drowning out the quiet, the peaceful way.
The heart's true path, obscured from view,
Buried beneath the mind's relentless to-do.

Oh, to silence the endless chatter,
To find peace amidst the mental clatter.
To trust the intuition, the heart's gentle call,
And let go of need to know it all.

For in the stillness, the answers may lie,
Beyond the confines of the overthinking mind.
To live, to breathe, to simply be,
The greatest gift, from overthinking, to be free.

Body Shaming

They look, they judge, they whisper and stare,
Casting harsh critiques without a care.
Flaws magnified, features dissected with glee,
As if the body's worth is theirs to decree.

"Too thin, too fat, too small, too tall',
The barrage of comments, a relentless thrall.
Insecurities planted, self-worth eroded,
As the soul's true beauty is cruelly corroded.

But beneath the skin, a story untold,
Of struggles and triumphs, of strength yet
untold.
A vessel that carries the weight of each day,
Deserving of kindness, not cruel dismay.

For whom are they to deem, what is right?
To dictate the shape, the size, the might?
Each body a canvas, a work of art,
Unique and precious, from the very start.

So let the critics speak, their voices ring,
While we stand tall, our worth we will sing.
For true beauty lies not in outward form,
But in the spirit that weathers each storm.

Embrace the skin you're in, with pride and
grace,
For you are worthy, just as you are, in this place.
Let not the judgments of others define,
The beauty shines, that is wholly mine.

Always The Poet and Never the Poem

I wield the pen, the words take flight,
Crafting verses that dance in the light.
Yet I remain, forever the scribe,
Observing the world, my soul as the guide.

I paint with language, emotions unfurled,
Capturing the beauty, the pain of this world.
But I am not the canvas, not the colors that
blend,
I am the artist, the one who must transcend.

The poems I write, they live, and they breathe,
Touching hearts of those who receive.
But I, the poet, forever unseen,
Trapped in the shadows, the in-between.

I long to be the poem, the verse that inspires,
To be the flame that ignites the soul's fires.
To be the muse, the very essence that sings,
Not just the hand that the quill deftly brings.

Alas, my fate is to be the creator,
The weaver of tales, the master narrator.
Forever the poet, never the poem,

Condemned to watch as my words find their
home.

A bittersweet burden, this role I must bear,
To craft the beauty, but never be there.
To be the architect, the builder of dreams,
Yet never the canvas where the masterpiece
gleams.

The Sting of Words

Cutting words, barbed and cruel,
Lashing out, a hurtful tool.
Meant to demean, to belittle and shame,
Leaving scars that are hard to tame.

Insults sting, they would the soul,
Chipping away at one's sense of control.
They erode self-worth, breed self-doubt,
Sowing seeds of fear, keeping us in.

For words have power, more than we know,
To lift or tear down, to heal or to blow.
Insults are arrows, aimed to destroy,
Robbing us of our peace, our inner joy.

They breed resentment, fuel anger and strife,
Tearing apart the fabric of human life.
Kindling division, sowing discord and pain,
Leaving us all the poorer, unable to regain.

Yet we have the choice, to rise above the fray,
To meet insults with grace, to find a better way.
To respond with compassion, to seek
understanding,

For only then can true healing and growth be
expanding.

Insults may wound, but they need not define,
Our worth as human beings, our light that can
shine.
Let us choose the path of empathy and care,
Uplifting one another, a world to repair.

Bad Dreams

Darkness falls, the mind takes flight,
Trapped in a realm of eerie fright.
Nightmares swirl, a twisted dance,
Tormenting the soul, leaving no chance.

Monsters lurk, their eyes aglow,
Chasing dreams into the unknown.
Panic rises, heart racing fast,
Desperate to wake, the nightmare will not last.

But dawn will break, the shadows flee,
Bringing solace, setting the mind free.
The bad dreams fade, its power undone,
As the light of day has finally won.

Though the night may bring fearful things,
The morning's light new hope it brings.
The mind can rest, the soul finds peace,
When the bad dream's torment at last does
cease.

False Whispers

Idle tongues, they never rest,
Spinning tales, they love the test.
Rumors fly, like birds on wing,
Feeding off the juicy sting.

Voices hushed, behind closed doors,
Painting pictures, nothing more.
Reputations torn asunder,
Leaving victims lost in wonder.

What drives this need to know?
To spread the word, to make it grow?
Is it boredom, or a thirst for power?
To watch the drama, hour by hour?

Yet in the end, what do we gain?
Broken trust, relationships in strain.
The thrill of gossip will fade,
Leaving scars that won't be swayed.

Finally Closing the Door

Echoes of the past still linger,
Memories cling like a stubborn finger.
Unresolved emotions, a tangled web,
Holding us back, refusing to ebb.

The door to closure, it beckons near,
Yet the path is shrouded, filled with fear.
To let go, to move on, to find release,
Requires courage, a journey to peace.

Each step forward, a battle to win,
Shedding the weight, the baggage within.
Facing the demons, the doubts, the pain,
Until closure we so long to attain.

The door swings open, a new dawn breaks,
Leaving behind the heartache it takes.
A sense of freedom, a weight lifted high,
As we embrace the chance to start anew, to fly.

Closure, the key to healing the soul,
Allowing us to become once more, whole.
A journey not easy, but one worth the fight,
To find the peace that shines in the light.

The Regrets

The weight of regret, a heavy burden to bear,
Haunting my steps, a shadow ever there.
Memories replay, a constant refrain,
Of choices made that caused such pain.

If only I had seen the path clearer,
Avoided the missteps that now bring me fear.
The what-ifs and should-haves, a torturous
dance,
Robbing the present of any true chance.

Yet in the darkness, a glimmer of light,
A chance to learn, to make things right.
To embrace the lessons this regret has taught,
And forge a future, with wisdom bought.

Though the past cannot be undone,
I'll move forward, toward a brighter sun.
Accepting the regret, but not letting it define,
For in this moment, a new path is mine.

Getting Older

With each passing year, the lessons accrue,
Experiences etched; perspectives renewed.
The youthful exuberance slowly gives way,
To a deeper understanding, a calmer sway.

The fires of ambition may burn less bright,
But in their place, a steadier, wiser light.
The race against time has long since been run,
Replaced by a journey a race that's won.

The body may weaken, the steps may slow,
But the mind grows richer, the spirit aglow.
Memories cherished, regrets left behind,
Age brings clarity, a peace of mind.

The world may see wrinkles and graying hair,
But within beats a heart, still young and fair.
For with growing older comes a priceless gain,
The wisdom to navigate life's joy and pain.

In the twilight years, a new strength takes hold,
Forged from the trials that life's path has told.
So let us embrace the gift of each new day,
And the lessons that growing old will convey.

The Things That Were Unsaid

In the spaces between the words we speak,
Lies a world of unspoken truths to seek.
The silence that lingers, pregnant with meaning,
Reveal the depths our voices are not reaching.

For sometimes, the most profound things we
feel,
Are the ones we cannot fully reveal.
The emotions that simmer beneath the surface,
Waiting to be understood, not just rehearsed.

It is in these moments of quiet reflection,
That we glimpse the heart's true complexion.
the unspoken longings, the unvoiced fears,
The unshared joys that bring both smiles and
tears.

For the unsaid holds a certain sacred grace,
A vulnerability that we must embrace.
It is the language of the soul, unbound by
speech,
Connecting us to truths we cannot fully reach.

Listen closely with open hearts and minds,
To whispers of the unsaid that our spirits find.
For in the spaces between the words we share,
Lies a wellspring of understanding, beyond
compare.

The unsaid speaks volumes, if we but take the
time,
To hear its quiet resonance, its melody sublime.
For in this realm of the unspoken, we may find,
The deepest connection of humankind.

Do You?

Do you hear whispers in the wind?
Do you feel the rhythm of the world spin?
Do you see the beauty all around?
Do you listen to subtle sounds?

Do you taste the sweetness of the air?
Do you smell the flowers blooming there?
Do you touch the heart with gentle hands?
Do you understand the silent demands?

Do you ponder life's great mysteries?
Do you dream of distant galaxies?
Do you seek the truth with an open mind?
Do you leave your worries behind?

Do you live each moment to the full?
Do you let your heart and soul be ruled?
Do you dare to follow your own way?
Do you seize the wonder of each day?

The question lingers, "do you?" they ask,
Inviting you to shed your mask.
To open, to feel, to see,
The wonders that hold life for thee.

Left Out

Watching from the sidelines,
As others have their fun.
Longing to be included,
To be part of the action, not just one.

The sting of exclusion,
A painful, hollow feeling.
Wondering what's wrong with me,
Why I'm not deemed worthy of revealing.

Seeing the laughter and connection,
Wishing I could join the fold.
Left out in the cold, alone,
My story yet to be told.

Insecurities creep in,
Doubting my worth and place.
Am I not good enough?
Not cool, smart, or popular enough to grace?

The desire to belong, to be accepted,
A universal human need.
Yet sometimes we're left on the fringes,
Our cries for inclusion unheeded.

Left out may sting in the moment,
But it's a chance to grow and thrive.
To carve my own path, my own story,
And ensure I'm never left out, but fully alive.

Nothing Changes

The tides may ebb and flow,
The seasons come and go.
But in our little world,
Nothing ever seems to unfurl.

The same old routines,
The familiar scenes.
Day in and day out,
No change, no doubt.

We used to have dreams,
Visions and schemes.
To grow and evolve,
Our love to revolve.

But now it's all the same,
No passion, no flame.
Just comfortable rut,
Where our spark has been shut.

We used to be alive,
Thriving, not just surviving.
But now it's a struggle,
To keep our love juggle.

Nothing changes, nothing new,
Just the same old, same old, through and
through.
The stagnant shores of our relationship,
Leaving us feeling adrift.

Is this what love is meant to be?
A lifeless, monotonous sea?
We must find a way to reignite,
Before our love fades out of sight.

The Perfect Place

In a secluded valley, hidden from the world,
Lies a place of wonder, its beauty unfurled.
Towering mountains reach up to the sky,
Their snow-capped peaks piercing the clouds on
high.

A crystal-clear lake, its water serene,
Reflects the majesty of the landscape's green.
Lush forests surround, their canopy dense,
Providing a sanctuary, a tranquil expanse.

The air is crisp and clean, untrained by strife,
Filled with the symphony of nature's sweet life.
Birdsong echoes, a melodic refrain,
As gentle breezes whisper a soothing refrain.

Time seems to slow in the haven of peace,
Where the soul can find solace, the mind finds
release.
No worries or trouble, no stress or dismay,
Just the simple joys of each passing day.

This is the perfect place, a realm of delight,
Where the spirit can soar, unencumbered and
light.

A sanctuary of beauty, harmony and grace,
The essence of life, the ultimate perfect place.

29

Been Here Before

The familiar ache, the well-worn path,
Another chance to feel love's aftermath.
The signs were there, the red flags waved,
Yet still, I let my heart become enslaved

I've walked this road, I've shed these tears,
Replaying memories of past fears.
The cycle spins, the pattern clear,
Another love, another heartache, year after year

Why do I keep returning to this place?
Allowing hurt to once again erase
The lessons learned, the wisdom gained,
As I fall victim to the same refrain.

But deep within, a voice calls,
Urging me to heed love's clarion calls.
For maybe, just maybe, this time will be
different,
The ending not so painfully recurrent.

So, I take a breath, and choose to try,
Knowing full well I may again cry.
For the hardest part is facing what's come
before,
And still daring to open my heart once more.

Who Says?

Who says the path must be paved and straight?
That success looks a certain way, on a timetable
set?
Who decrees the rules we must abide,
The limits we must stay confined inside?

Who claims there's only one right way to live?
That our dreams must fit a mold they'll approve
and give?
Who dares to judge what's worthy, what's not
Dismissing the journey we've fought and
fought?

Well, I say screw their expectations, their norms.
I'll blaze my own trail, weather any storms.
Who are they to dictate how I should be?
I'll write my own story, live life authentically.

Let the doubters and naysayers have their say.
I'll keep moving forward, come what may.
For I am the author of my own destiny,
And I'll never let anyone else define me.

www.ingramcontent.com/pod-product-compliance
Lightning Source LLC
La Vergne TN
LVHW010939200726
843509LV00013B/2248